Rumored Animals

Rumored Animals

poems by

Quinn Latimer

Dream Horse Press
www.dreamhorsepress.com
Editor: J.P. Dancing Bear

Dream Horse Press
Post Office Box 2080
Aptos, California 95001-2080
U.S.A.

Latimer, Quinn
   Rumored Animals
     p.116

      ISBN 978-1-935716-13-6
      1. Poetry

10 9 8 7 6 5 4 3 2 1

First Edition

Cover: Jennifer West, *Dawn Surf Jellybowl Film (16mm film negative sanded with surfboard shaping tools, sex wax melted on, squirted, dripped, splashed, sprayed and rubbed with donuts, zinc oxide, cuervo, sunscreen, hydrogen peroxide, tecate, sand, tar, scraped with a shark's tooth, edits made by the surf and a seal while film floated in waves - surfing performed by Andy Perry, Makela Moore, Alanna Moore, Zach Moore, Johnny McCann - shot by Peter West - film negative sanded by Mariah Csepanyi, Andy Perry and Jwest),* 2011. Still from a color film in 16mm transferred to HD video. Commissioned by the Contemporary Arts Forum, Santa Barbara, California. Courtesy MARC FOXX, Los Angeles, and Vilma Gold, London.

Cover design: Sarah Leugger

Table of Contents

IV.

V.

For my mother, Blake Amelia Latimer (1953–2007)
Without whom, never—

And for my father, Irv Katz
For whom the same holds true.

"The sight of that abrupt and truncated animal padding softly across the quadrangle changed by some fluke of the subconscious intelligence the emotional light for me. It was as if someone had let fall a shade."

—Virginia Woolf

I.

Brush Fire

This ravishing is not
the cipher in the grass

occluding the sun.
Meadow singed soon

enough. It is the perfect
dismembering of my

body that I do so well,
each part singing itself

into relief against grass
that is high and blonde

as a girl. I hide inside
her, spelling myself

this way, spelling myself
that. On the cool ground

beneath a tree, my mouth
lies torn and bruised

among the fruit. My face
is beautiful without it,

closed and white as a moon.
Summer is cinder the way

I live her. My art is colder.
I remember how it tasted

like metal. I go toward
my arms where they are

wrapped around each other
in the sun, and I rub them

together until each falls
to fire, and then I call the wind.

Intelligence

I wake with a thirst for your body.
Stay in bed longer trying to create

it around me. What is intelligence
cast off into sea? I dive off some future

boat into clear green water, chanting
this is me, this is me. The bears asleep

in their distant winter charge the invisible
man again and again, and do not wake.

Under the sea, I look up and comprehend
light spiraling out from a golden head.

Know I must reach it, but wait a bit
longer. In this water, I am absent, entire.

The spike driven into a fallow field
and forgotten, does not cower under

shrieking wind. With sorrow it seeks
the earth around it, its metal leaking

bit by bit, red and then black, and forever.

Slander

Of your rumor animal
I know: its coat of wool

and searing bloat-speak
of summer, when words

wear looser, talk more limber.
In winter, with haunches

stiffer—the noise cold
and sober—your animal

recites our names better:
sister, lover, daughter, scour.

Spoken thus, shaken from
sumac by the throat of your

beast, we fall, grabby
as starfish eager for extension,

for elaboration. We are your
animal's violent instinct

to speech, dusky titles
of season, the inherited habit

of slander. Our names
bristle its fur, open its mouth.

Your pet, sir, is speaking.

My West

Not the thing of my sympathy and its stop
nor yours, I am always the compass to you,

my undecided star, my West. Nothing stops this.
Years ago, I considered the mouth's station, thinking it suited me,

gaping and omniscient. Knew nothing and became it.
Now, loose and awful, the sun burns through the trees,

seeing everything. What was once me speaking
is blister beneath the leaves' light-shifting.

I was not supposed to be all need. All want, all speed.
As a child, my memory quickened—experience

did not lead but followed—and came before the wish
I was sent to the river to swallow.

Delineation of Light and Water

Inside the desire, it was like standing in a field of fluorescent

light. Everything was lit the same by my idea of you: the birds,

the grass, the sky. This was your importance: that you might

illuminate each thing equally. It was also like those summer

days when the heat outside seems to match exactly the heat

of my body, so that moving along I cannot tell where the air ends

and I begin. In truth, I am not outside the desire yet,

but imagine that it is like the time I was swimming laps

in Ventura, and a boy left his lane, dove to the floor of the pool,

and began swimming underneath me, slowly rising until his back

brushed my chest. Still swimming, my hands cutting through

the water around him, I stared down at the water-pale body

miming my own, and he turned his head upward toward mine

and grinned. We swam this way to the wall, turned, and kicked off

into different directions. There is nothing about your body

I miss, and yet staring down into the wavering water, I cannot think

of anything but its appearance, the finer fluency of its absence.

The Fragments of Swennen

Do we speak now concerning the art of Swennen
Or concerning living everyone?

That does not veil Swennen, reveals he.
Wind ensures the rest.

For the Swennen has a high figure, the gravitation plays a role—
The artist such as builder, in with its hands and arm brandishing—

The artist as lover, as operator, in with heart and mouth
Brandishing. Tools striking like a clock: on the hour, on the hour.

Studio like a page, pale and distant, that Swennen takes his pencil to.
Studio like a sun, pale and distant, that Swennen takes his pencil to.

Helicopter that lopes across the canvas like a bird, half mad.
Scissor of its wings:

Clip.
Clip.
Clip.

Glass that stains the painting: half silence, half blur.
Thought winging it through the stuttering, gesturing

Air. Swennen stopped, soaked, storied,
Famishing. Feeling, like a watercraft, lands

To some splashing.

At Swennen that vanalles can be—

vanalles
van alles

of everything.

Agriculture

Preparation does not hold water like a bowl,
it holds water like a mouth. As dresses are

boned and broken. Restless, my horses move
away from me, gleaning something to eat,

hooves scraping softly at grass. The wind
blows hot air across damp loam; in between

we are stopped. In the green plots further, figures
stoop for strawberries and the ocean does not

go hungry. Is caution a rehearsal? Are those
freeways of concrete and apple? I am less

than this performance of departure, this dent
in a field of faded fabrics and nothing to eat.

Identical homes inure in the distance: peach
and bleached. I know now (I am not sure

I always knew): we will have no escort. My song
is short, keeling. What is this other singing?

The Gift

We drive the desert's
reticence. From mountains
the white anger

of windmills, which regard me sharply
and then not at all: I am flooded
with their indifference,

its pleasure. O dazzling, O damage:
Drought drugs the air
with air and I am here,

valley of Joshua Trees
that crook broken arms at me,
offering up their disfigurement.

All morning our speed quickening
like a photo book
flipped through quickly: frame frame frame.

Music fills my head like fog
as trees are skinned by animals
in search of water. Their skin

hangs down stiff as paper
round the wrested waists of old men, clothes
scissored off by a hospital orderly.

My lover ignores
their gaping regatta; thinks it separate
as if by glass. But I watch them.

Born again each day under the
ruthless blue government
of sky. O sluts, O alien race:

thirsty as rodents my eyes drink in
your display. You wave
grotesquely, as if to say:

I gave you away
each time. I give you away now.

After-Work Swim at the Thunderbird Motel

That would be our pool, that shaky stunner: blue-born
and unnerving as the earring left at its studied edge,

untitled and unattached. Pure, its pearly glint a glance
that both rectifies and grants a certain slash-like

blindness (the angle of light go shunt go slant)—
such is the pupil of the estimating cat, she so

gracefully inured to the pleasure of taking one's
cure in the mineral baths. Us, we shiver and lower,

we cool to the chemical slide of our hips. Thus
your smile's shimmer begins its luminous. Its streak

across glassy surface, pressing outward in half-moon
or noon-sun ripples that acquire and acquire. It is

its light that impresses me so, casting wet-dark
shadow as watermark, pale and voluptuous as the

inside of a wrist. And so my consent, I give it: here
and here you go, anything, darling, but then

away I move, water disarming any dulled
appreciation, unmoved and removing what

○

work we completed, by which I mean the one
hundred untitled sculptures we cleaned today.

Aluminum milled and ecstatic, was metallic but
also was mirrors was voids was transparent,

was all those in rows and rows. Now to the breeze
slipping on like a turban, which the semi's bring

to this highway Riviera. Their engines massive
and lowered as the god's head in his workshop, tools

slipped, back slumped, ache a child or a helmet
made, and behind what he cradles is cargo pressing

past our splash our float, and you are laughing inside
each truck that passes, and are here, holding

my ankles—and then to release—and the deep end
is yours and the shallow end yours, as in watery,

weightless carousel I exist in each of these places
with you. But with a cease and desist order, by which

I mean, *Mein Lieber*, you are holding me under. And a bit
too long. Just a bit. But the sculpture that stands

forgotten, clean as us, bathed by us to refraction,
to distraction in its grid of mirror-blue, what

○

if anything does it rue? Brevity of our season here?
Lack of flood? Cold patter of our kisses artless?

Which is what I—Oh, my newly chemical mind
is fantastic, thanks. And the trucks are too, swimming

past my floating form set adrift as just another
sun-carved floe in slippery apprenticeship

to your virtue. It is your eyes' violet pools casting
phosphorescent nets that our apprentice clings to.

And if my eyes of red are true, are stung, yes, that's
true too, I'm stung, inside this too coherent pool

by you and you and—Is it better to bathe the mind
or the body after the art ablutions are through? Wistful,

my long silver arm snakes its way in figure-eights
to you who would cherish its baited route. So hear

my hushed admonition its curated admiration this
underwater plea in intervals to brace. Against curving

concrete walls, below candy-colored bobbing lane
dividers that exist simply to dive under: again, aquatic,

the echoing cry of *Mein Lieber*: we might stay.

Diorama

The sun forcing itself across
the sky is a type of scraping.

As is all obligatory movement.
Inside my chest an animal

pawing relentlessly. What
I know: not the heaviness but

the terrible accuracy of
its hooves. Also the delicacy.

It thrashes movingly inside
the diorama of my chest.

My ribs some white instinct
to fall against. Like stripes

of light you move from faith
to myth just as quick. As

this scene—its superb action
of error—is both smaller

and larger than my life. And
the animal *will* remember the bit,

the cold copper religion of it,
and cannot (for you) let go.

Ein Baum im Feld

A tree turning, sweeping, sheering
clear of its surroundings, environs
intelligent to the stranger standing,
stooping, describing the field's
distance, as it were, in boots, torn
jacket, tousled hair, the tree hasn't
slept in a week, it cannot move,
hair that springs forward as branches
reach and so divisible require electric,
oh strung with lights that do not work,
oh lights that blink and blare. Oh, ein
baum im feld, it was my friend, I knew
her well, she was my mother, I had
a sister, there was this stranger
standing sober as a tree, slouching
against field, sloughing through mud
as it rained, it snowed, grasses they grew
she grew but with no water went
blonde, a dry yellow that burnt and
swayed where the wind it found her
moored, found my stranger, found me
felled by grasses somewhat fulsome,
kicking at pastures wet as blood after
some bandaging storm, my boots
so scuffed, so soft, like kittens they
sniffed at puddles of red earth, they ran
in fields of antelope grass, but with no
mother to chase them, no soother to
grace what we call "the two of them,"
like boots they strolled they stopped,
they fled they fell, the fallow weather
it wore them well, and went and willed
there be some everything-changing

storm, so I willed her back, mother
we mourn, me and my sister, such
a soft kitten, my boots, my boots, ein
baum im feld, a tree im feld, a figure
this horizon some ground or dirt-flood
of grasses maybe scattered with kittens,
boot 1, boot 2, clawing or stomping,
threading the field, dreaming the feld, maybe
im feld, maybe im feld maybe im feld.

Fluorescents

Bits of bone and the green wigs of trees, fluorescent. I smooth
down the pleats of the evening, which unfold and fall around
my knees, those bald, blank men, narrow-eyed, obscured, and
my skirt, that of night, sounds a long, low chime—when I leap
up to greet your ghost. I had written it a letter. The page glowed
in the desert's dusty, accelerating dark. It had laid in my lap like
a pneumatic's hand, romantic. Now it sat in the bowl of a yucca,
at the base of the flower that fled upwards and died, each bloom
clenched like a child's dirty fist, like a series of bells the damaged
white of bone. Rung by no one, alone in the vast arcade of air.
The sky is exhausting, ghost. It covers everything. Downtown,
a hum of trucks and Stetsons tipped, and the slim towering of
streetlamps, those tall, hopeful girls waiting at every corner,
whose dreams, blooming as a radical, spectral orange, we tried
to shoot out last night. If the line of cottonwoods set along the
highway shimmer austerely, my missives are trucks, perfecting
the art of the one-handed wave, before speeding away. If the
museum sits on the blondest plain above town, jackrabbits flash
on and off like white fluorescents among the mulberry trees.
In the old gas station, teenagers hold hands and pray before
their pizza, baseball murmurs whispering statistically from the
corner. Outside, night drops its photographer's black cloth. The
sculpture considers only itself, forgetting its station in the space
it was asked by its maker to determine. The gods' hands leap
away from their material. March winds bear forth, touching
each small light like a face made vague by the thrown-back cloak
of evening. And the shadows of birds playing the long, fretted
necks of trees. Hear them. Hear me. I made myself rare of your
requiring, ghost. See: you won't find me here. I am everywhere.

Your Portrait as Various Bodies of Water

This desert is a roan horse.
Under its thin, sand-colored coat

pools of purple and red reflect
mountains worrying the perimeter.

My mirage, my wavering fever—
your eyes are this color: unmoving

water. Against blue, your head turns
dazzling, is dull wheat rippling

as when we compare it to water.
The sky has so many names for itself.

I wait for you to
sound the troubled lake of your mouth.

Watch your eyes dam and darken
when I speak.

I am spooked by our ruin. You watch this
from a great height, unimpressed.

The rock where you choose to rest
is massive. I would have worn

it in my mouth. You are uninterested
in warmth. Day deepens

its pigments, the sun circling us
like a dog. Some rivers are bodies

and will not stop. I start at the top
of the sea, that is—anywhere.

Love Comes to the Cracker Factory

Was the flood mouse in your garret,
my love, parroting on about the merits
of a certain love of water. Soaked,

you spoke, essaying darlings
like daggers, eye to the rising
tide. Which swept the floorboards, finally

reaching the mouth of the tiger, black-
velveted, that stared opaquely from the west
wall, and which hung completely on some

obscure aesthetic delivery of your
suburban (*superb*) devising. Oh, love, I staggered
at your choices: this tiger, the water, me.

I did not think of drowning. I thought
of our meeting: the train and its sidelong
glance of river; my enacted slumber

as your mouth found my hair and love
began. Love, it began there. I swear
that it did, when detrained, we walked

the wide corridors of the museum, a former
cracker factory filled with austere
artifacts gleaned from the anti-narrative.

The paintings about perfection made
us pause; their story was light, was it not?
The room illumined by the sober ecstasy

of its almost Puritan maker. Who, pictured
on the cover of a book of her writings
(my mother gave it to me for Christmas, see:

it all connects), sits hands in lap, white
smocked, in a rocking chair that is stopped,
with a white grid behind her, burning bright.

Although ideas about perfection make me
dubious, I let the paintings move me so you
could watch. Ignoring my performance, *not*

to flatter my intelligence, you moved toward
the gallery of sculpture fashioned from metal,
from some harbored memory of ships' gestures.

Surface rose everywhere above us, red rusted
steel, the feel of which was cold, turning my eye
cold and analytical. Until it fell on you.

A Chronology of Color in the Desert

SILVER

The donkey lady inscribes herself, her animal, to silvering
desert night. Voluminous dark flares out
like a dress around her. She keeps to the edge

of slim highway flung across the high plain
like an arm in sleep. Questions distance themselves
from her like stars.

RED

dents in the sky that take her study: blink,
blare. A maker laid this path to the cold deserted
body, desert floor. He pauses as she rides

slow as a prayer across his work. Clears
his throat. His workshop is warm today.
His tools still. The careful solitude

of a car approaches a kill
smeared like a mouth
across tender asphalt glitter and vast

BLACK

birds bloom their blue-black
many-petaled flower, rise and hover
and unravel. Beat

VIOLET

sky liquid. The maker is used to this. Dark
tape of wings unwound, the film stopped. The birds
drop back in, mouths working like acid, the film begins.

But the lady and her animal. Why does he feel
it is his throat they travel? Fluency of his hands
they trap and catch? And latch

of his understanding to

RUST

I to rust and you also.
For when she stops to sleep it will be
face down, with privacy of a swimmer.

The highway's heat a kind
of water. Though not for
transformation. For swimming the tangled

GREEN

harbor of her long, damaging dream.
This exclusion has always been my wonder, yes. What are we
that we find her? There, under a

BLUE

tarp, Mexican skirt of many
colors. Highway a nerve in

YELLOW

coursing past. Though thorns stud the coat
of her companion. Whom she layers in the

BLACK

tinsel bags of the mad.

Flare

Because horses of the desert
carry a darker coat so they should
not burn white along the dunes

Because horses of the desert
ride smaller hooves like infant skulls
left as a long bone trail in sand

Because horses of the desert
hold a plumage of tail high
behind and taut necks shudder

Because horses of the desert
sewn trembling into a wide
blue sky will never ride

Because horses of the desert
what I love I have betrayed
Light flames the thinnest skin

Because horses of the desert
dark nostrils flare there is
a shrove of dust some coming storm

The Eels

After a photograph by Francesca Woodman

Inside a large porcelain bowl
the eels move one against
the other, two black rainbows
coiled to match the curve of their

perimeter. The eels' taut arch is
repeated in the body of water beyond
their bowl. A slim hip artlessly
breaking the surface; the hip—that wing—

an island of strict shore and law.
A soft reef of thigh keeps
the deeper pastures at bay,
and a path of hair, dark as kelp,

sweeps in and out, docile to the moon's
maneuverings. The body presses against
the water as the eels to each other,
the same comb rippling each sentence

as the bodies stretch it farther.
Were the bodies to rise—the eels
dancing along the lip of their bowl,
flopping violently to its shore;

or the girl to pull up her length,
to step against sky, her body sure—
then I could leave the scene and live
without words to describe it.

No. My body, like theirs, has fallen
out of such movement and into water
where all borders are defined by
a body and the water lapping against it.

Whose hands hold this picture?
Whose eyes? The coiled eels circle the blue
water of my iris, tighten around the black
pupil at the shrinking center of the world.

II.

Chekhov's Photograph

It's awful how easily women give
themselves away to men, said my friend,
to whom I had given myself away

twice. I was in the middle of the second
terrible giving when he said this. Outside
car alarms began in sharp chorus: *no, no, no.*

His face turning to ember busied itself
with distance. Feeling my way through
the air, I sat at the small, scarred piano

that sulked near the window. Thought of only
the feral cats rubbing up against the stucco
of his house, the awful orange claw of their bodies.

Virginia Woolf said of Chekhov:
"We must cast about to find out
where in these stories the emphasis lies."

The cats, etc. Yes or no. No. The mock
irony of his understanding (yes) and the attendant
instrument (no). Desire stuttering out of the room (perhaps).

I once searched Chekhov's photograph for what
was most emphatically *him*: turned-
up collar of the narrow double-breasted

coat, puckered poof of sleeves, the fore-
finger of his right hand resting lightly
on a thin, shiny cane. Leaning back easily

on an elbow, his eyes pressed into me.
On the porch behind, an empty chair
sat awkwardly above him, as though it were

a painting intimidated by its owner. He was
a sharp dresser, that Doctor. His kind eyes,
they pecked at my face. We do not always want

understanding. It can also be a form of betrayal. For instance:
In a dream I have over and over, my mother
and I rest on the roof of a house in the middle

of a turquoise sea. As the rip begins to pull
me out to where the water is darker, she must
swim me in. The house's strict minimalism

infers my fear of enclosure (perhaps), but could also
mean my love of the lines. Waking from this dream,
shame is always what dresses me. And this might be

the emphasis, yes? Not the salt that streaks her arms.
My mother has always said that I hang on
too long. That in this way, I am like my father.

◯

In the story where Woolf lost her footing at
"a long gray fence studded with nails," I was struck
by Chekhov's understanding of Gurov:

"He always seemed to women different
from what he was, and they loved in him not
himself, but the man whom their imagination

created and whom they had been seeking
all their lives; and afterwards, when they saw
their mistake, they loved him nevertheless.

And not one of them had been happy with him."
I say struck deliberately, because, as after
a slap, I was left with that burning sensation

coupled with a feeling of ice. Gurov found love
with "The Lady with the Pet Dog," but why?
And she, Anna, was not happy with him,

but like those women before her, she did not
seek him for happiness. She sought him for love.
But what made her love real and not

a creation of her imagination? Was his love for her
simply his imagination come suddenly loose,
like some steamer off Yalta released from its pier

and set adrift into fog, and so into wild, terrible
being? These are very elementary questions, but
they interest me. When one is left alone

in love, these questions become important.
Behind my friend's house, where I sat tracing
wet-glass rings on a piano, an alley glittered of glass,

catching the light from a sunset that had dropped
its red cape over the desert basin of the city. It was
Chekhov's demonstration that Gurov's new

and fuller understanding of himself and Anna
had come only with his love for her, that worried
me. True knowledge of oneself and others

can take place outside of love. The doubleness
of understanding that Chekhov located within love—
as Gurov understood that, for him, there was no human

more important in the world than Anna, this little,
provincial woman—also occurs outside of it.
For instance, sitting there in my friend's room,

as he circled me with his new wash of remove,
his understanding parsing my brain into
unrelated fragments, I also saw us both quite clearly.

○

It was like standing outside a small corral,
and watching a horse circle its perimeter
over and over, the sound of hooves in canter

coming closer, becoming harsh, and then
receding, and then again. When the horse
suddenly stops, nostrils flared and breathing hard,

the heat discernible in the dust that fills the air,
and then spins into the opposite direction
and begins its circling anew, one knows the change

of direction will occur before the horse ever
slides to a stop. Because watching from
the perimeter, one cannot help but be the horse

as well as oneself. The understanding does not come
from love always. It can come from proximity.
My friend, my lover, began to circle closer,

seeing in me, what? Himself (perhaps). Outside, the cats
began shrieking of the electricity of their bodies.
Words made tiny fists (yes) inside my mouth.

III.

Fuel

Let it burn. Get rid of the fuel.
The house is warm but the walls are cool.
To the touch, to the touch,
The hand like a match, the body
Like a screen, the cheek a pool, whatever may be
Behind the door: fire, fever, love her,
Leave her, but not to fire, not to fire,
Your thoughts that hurry
Towards her, steps so light like leaves
Whose shadows are blurring, but your ankles,
Thin as tinder, they're burning, and the sand
It slows the long season of you, unfolding,
While the water it pulls you, and the mountains
Fever and flower wide crimson
Petals, sharp orange pistils, yellow buds that mouth
They love you, they love you,
As they score the foothills, writ them
With ash, black cursive letters that thrall
That kill you, such *tall* letters,
They read as tombs to the trees buried
Beneath, also borne beneath, also borne above
In ash that fills the sky like tears, that fills
Your face "like tears" like leaves
Gray and burning, blurring the cool
Slide of your cheek, empty
Pool, concrete and absence, and the children
Who rest, at the bottom, they watch
Orange flowers flaming above like heaven,
This brother and sister, their mouths are closed, eyes

Are open, language has left them
Like a lover, like a mother has
Fled them, so they roam but not resist
A concrete floor, no, not to rise, not to rise,
The walls so steep, so curved, so round
As a mother's body in sleep,
Her "female nude" her heavy modernity,
But she is not still nor here she walks
The fire-flowering hills, scorching their sides
With her black poems, and far
From her heavy steps, and below her world
Of ash, it's here they live now, waiting for flood
Or fathers to find them, but alone, alone,
While her words whisper across the still:
Let it burn. Get rid of the fuel.

Mineral Violence

The vast sadness of my family
is an ocean rehearsing its sorrow
against the intractable night.

By light we are careful, bruised
and beautiful as script, hair tangled
from evening's beating. We stoop

to inspect the night's debris
and do not recognize black
half-hearts of shell (that are ours),

wool of kelp. The jetty's battered
knuckles count the endless waves
rolling in. Watching birds drawn

as graphite on sky, we forget
our night deaths. I do not understand
this, nor our strange thick hair, only

that I am of it. Wheat of my mother,
father's beard of bees: I am their
provided. O mineral violence

release their salt traffic, their
hovering at sea. I will exist.
Give them what they want.

The Invention

"…the parents seem to be dreaming the child
and the child seems to be inventing them."
—Diane Arbus

I fashion each from salt: give them eyes,
static hair, sighs of mouths, hands for work

and measure. I suture each against weather
though their eyes are made of sea and hair

of roads for leaving. I shape small bones
of driftwood, snow, and sand, and with these

slight flutes I deceive all predators, for their middles
I fill with metal. I dab their skin with resin, cloak

their eyes with air. I leave the clouds' wool
unused. Leave the aching lung at rest.

My hands falter. Longing runs through
their veins. Fingers twist their shining hair.

Doubt shadows the wide O of their mouths
and dives in forever. They come to life.

In their bodies I see a fever. It is a dream.
They have a child who lasts forever.

Black silk of eyes I cannot stitch
closed: They do not know what I have done

I have not done right.

Inexpert

In the long afternoon of your arm
I construct a sound. It removes itself
immediately, like a bell, and is heard
sounding deeply some rooms away.

We lay together, against that tolling.
Yet somewhere, far from my terrible
eyes, I am whole and dreaming of
an island four or five years away,

and beautiful in its established future.
Birds with feet like old, withered hands
touch down briefly off its shore, small
compasses of water fleeing concentrically

at their entry. Gray shoals of wings
suddenly spread and flap, inexpert
at terror. A sound has seized them and
they rise, removing themselves over

and over, infinitely. Is this not my island,
terror? Are these not my animals fleeing?
Like heat we hover near the ceiling,
sound, its future, displacing us further.

We round off, ever a briefer number.

Lady in the Lake

The fever broke. The trees began to flower.
From their mouths a lurid alliteration
of petals streamed: salamander, sentient rose,

a velvety slice of violet-bruised white
so creamy it seemed to come off a sun-laden truck.
I tried to sense my feelings about the thing. The water,

the travel, the lover, the weather. The ribbon of dischord
that would hold it all together. As a willow washed
her pale green hands along the rocks, white fluorescents

of boats—at slippery dream in their docks—flickered
in the shade of her long, lime hair. And the water darkened.
I shook off the lake. Fish tore through the trees.

What had been fire—forest, fuel, finally fever—now
froze me, the cooling, temperate shores of my body, fixed me
in its coldest glance. The blossoms, without flush of blood's

administering map, were ice, were Lucite jaws admiring
their bone structure in the water's mirror. If I said
I had understood that the lake was a woman,

I lied. She kept her sex hidden from me all that
long week. I bathed, swam, wandered the watery corridors
of her fathomless blue haul. Pulled myself out

so her touch beaded my darkening skin
into diamonds, which cut and glittered like mother's
suicidal mutterings. A necklace of kisses to sequence the spine.

I was at the lake and she would die.
Who? The lady liquidly grooming herself under
glassy, unimpeachable surface? The melancholy willow—

ever the widow, the maiden, the sorrow sainted—with her deft
fairytale ablutions? Or my far westerly mother?
It was all a long, late-summer drama. Shadows lean

and limpid and outrageous. Didn't the sky know?
It wrapped itself in blue, then black. Lucite tears stitched
like rhinestones to its cape, catching light from the lake's

long, mystifying look, and final scream, and splash.

Idols That Did Call and Call
and Call Your Name

At the scourge of the river I found you.
Bottles and two small dogs beside.

At your head and foot stacked books
Stood like idols, their regarding, angular figures formed

From volumes fell from the sky. The book-lined sky:
It fell. Over the mountains: fire that went

All the way to the ocean. My brother and I would take
The freeway through the valley to find you.

To leave you, we drove through the valley.
My father called to say the coast was burning. Take

The valley, he said. Where were you
All this time? With your bottles and two small dogs

Beside. Humming some tune
Along the scourge of the river. Your head propped up

On one hand. Hair of wheat falling round. And eyes of
Practiced silt, regarding. What were you

Singing? The plurals were all wrong. It was
A blues song. The neon ache of your voice

Moved over the water, gilding the shore
Orange with its ragged, beautiful

Scrawl. I loved you there: at the scourge
Of the river. When we went down to the river

You were still alive. Pacing, dreaming, tossing
Stones for the dogs. Your heart like a fist: opening,

Closing, pounding the shore, breaking
The idols. In its grasp, the world: a river, the

Ocean, some mountains, and fire. And two children calling
You down from the water. Down from the valley.

Down from the freeway that cuts across the fields
With its dull, damaging thrum. Down from the bottles leaning

Brokenly against each other. Down from the shattered
Idols that did call and call and call your name.

Dreamscape, Deadscape

My mother was one. I
Was two. What sum did we make?
What took, what take?

The man behind me furiously
Touching himself. Obedient dog at his side
Like a statue. Like one of those marble-immobile

Things at the gates of hell or a river.
In my dreams after, a man fed his cock
Into the mouth of a woman, then cut out

Her tongue (this might have come
From a Hungarian novel I once put down).
My mother stood near, thinking there

On the overpass of a freeway
Coursing like a red river through the hell
Of California. My mother with her head in her hands

In some room after, thighs smeared with blood.
Such dreams, what do they take?
What rook, what stake?

A man appearing calmly, his cock in his hand.
Darkness, a figure, and a door: obtuse city, unseeing.
There, in that deadscape, my father dead too.

In such dreams I know only this—deaths of those
Who made me, stones ascribing
Indiscriminate waters. But I will wake

To my father, will not to my mother. Not ever
Again. So. She was one. I made two. Let us
Forget this week. Forget this year.

The one that begins and continues its dear
Turns without her turning each day over
In her astonishable mind. Turning such sand as there

May be with her good, rough feet.
Turning these dreams of damage
Along with her forward, famished

Motion, that which was instantaneous—
The crab-crawl out, the thunderclap, beauty—
Insatiable, unsustainable.

Which the recent river murmurs of
As I trawl its fluorescent waters for dreams of her,
Taking and tearing the little paper tongues,

Painted bright as fish, which offer themselves but not relief.

To Your Dulled Wintering Body

Seagulls swoop above snow-covered
roofs that stretch out like lawns—

like desire, touching everything—outside
this window. Your mouth does not cover

your face like a hand. What made you
think that all the time? Words and their foal,

asleep on the hill, lie unaware. Could you—
but you always could, burning without

experiment in the shorter, darker room.

Short Report on Night

Stay still for the twelve-hour exposure.

Fit my hips into your hands. Hold

still. We of prayers examine the pictures

later. The blurs are where our bodies were.

They are the story of a love and the fence we

dragged there. The naked back and the help

offered: *You are not as filthy as I had hoped.*

Plaintive

In October, I was his
pharmaceutical. His red, his
blue. I went down

so easily. Held up to light
I was flecked with gold
and liquid as some

summertime. To my city
he brought the taste of lime
and to myself I was

not strange. Within his fever-pitch
I was apart and mine. Across
the river, we reversed

our scripts and almost kissed.
Then we did. The white
lights that dressed the bridge

were opiates, echoing
past our car in soft
focus spots. Our driver

watched the plaintive markers
of our mouths, shifting
in the dark—and I smiled,

generously. The eyes, from their
slant bejeweled mirror, recited:
you, you, you. This left me

curious for days. Almost fall, my science
wore into winter. He went away
and returned, nervous

as his earthquake weather. In December
there were others in
his dispensary. He took us

quickly, *with water—*
and we went down
without remedy.

Small Fires

My father was a runner,
and fashioned me of wood
and spark. Always burning,
I was the small fire
that slept in his truck
as he drove us into the black
and home. Mother, surrounded
by her dogs, yelling at
the river, continues
climbing her inexplicable
impassable mountain, but only in
my body, not the world's.
Her hair the bright yellow
of relief, it brought her
none. My brother then
a stone I could not see
for the water. December
and I am one. Slipping
in and out of the sheath
of their memory. Their necessity
rips me, it turns like a knife
against azure. Dazzling.
Though the slant, passionate storms
of their lives move over
my thoughts like studies of cloud,
I am lower. Round as the face
of a clock, orange as the moon
I have become: harvest, mask.
The brevity of their bodies
is not beautiful. It bewilders
me. I am strange for it,
their magnificent leaving.
Started in summer, by winter
they were gone: animals

who sought nothing in the night
because they did not exist
except in my conjuring.
How lithe this life. Wrested, less.
If I am here. If I am.

Anticipatory Landscape

In color your sleep is red. It is hunger that does this

            to paper lungs

bright as a lantern and floating down a river, waving

      to shore, those stung.

The hover of winter and your hip's thin grin of bone

            fell forward

in labor, an unrequited night to sorrow, but to spring

      it lashed back.

The animals left penned between this crimson dream

            and strict season

are only shadows, white eyes of what you did

      see first.

Fathers

To think I could have
sprung from your head

like that other daughter—
a headache in armor.

If I could have ceased
work on my helmet,

I should have, caused
you not the pain,

I should have, and let
my hair—worn like a

receiver of information—
spring away

from my head, roots
searching for soil.

Though It Be Foreign, Though It Be Terrible

Water pools the roof into mirrors
thin as any, the storm lilting

itself into something lighter,
still horizontal across the buildings,

sounding softly as through gauze.
Telephone lines make neat equations

against the sky. Birds add their dull
erasure as so many marks on white.

With wings washed by distance
their roosting thoughts breast measure,

odd glances taped to the horizon.
Their desire is fettered like any other,

forced to accept the season though it be
foreign, though it be terrible. This

is not terrible, to tremble so, wings
locked, feet threading the razor wire

keeping them afloat. The current within
carries a halting conversation of "please"

and "no" through thin horizons of speech
which, though inexplicable, are familiar

as the design these birds will make later,
a mosaic for me, and for them the required

lapse into movement, the posture of flying.

Noon

After Ingeborg Bachmann

Already the departures have been rehearsed,
the shores reserved—banners folded, put away
and lost. Already, today, I forgot your face.

Already the crowds have been dispersed,
left to wander the empty galleries of words
unspoken and shivering in white reflections.

Already the air has thinned with anticipation,
clouds pressing against that intention with blithe
malice, our modern feelings nearing an end.

Already, beneath the calculating sky, alien flowers
are blooming, studio lights hooding their progress.
Already they distract the light with their expert lies.

Already the skirt has matched its seam with a rip
spreading like water across silk, like animals moving
over a dark field toward a darker field of stars.

Already the ship hovers, a soft mark near the harbor,
the ashen shore unsure if it is approaching land
or leaving, its curved back—that long labor—rocking

in black water. Already I reach, longing through
this hour, parting sun and moon like hair. Already they draw
back with dislike, with fear. Already I am done here.

Black Words That Come Next

There's the world!
Said the poem,
The sad speculator.

Instruments of verification,
Telescope, goggles, child's soft spade,
Spread out across his maps,

Shifting like paper oceans
Heavy with the morose sisters of kelp beds.
The telescope stuck like an elbow

In the side of the world.
The speculator sighed.
I never thought you would die

Can also mean: I always thought you would
But not in that way.
Say it once:

If you were to leave
I thought it would be old and wise and by
My side. Or, as long intimated,

Middle-aged and anguished
And by your own hand.
But not by a boy named Chance—

Name my brother gave the dumb puppy
Born miraculously
Under our house on Ocean Avenue,

Which cried and grew—
But not this stranger, growing
Like a dull blade near the military base

Across town, who
Did kill you. The bag torn "cleanly" from your arm
Held Philip Roth's *Exit Ghost*.

Birthday present from my father.
And your notes about birds,
Poets, and your children scrawled

On yellow lined paper. Your
Yellow hair. More Margarete
Than Shulamith, but still: Your yellow hair.

It gives the speculator pause.
Makes his poem a torn, burned thing,
Like the maps that brittle and dismay.

Not clean as grief,
This. I've never liked
That saying. Too Christian, with its air

Of the genocidaire, and implication
Of death as ablution.
No, I think the poem

Is what was left after the fires
Ripped across the foothills
In the days after you died, and the solitary

Embers at the beach, in their careful
Rock circles. The poem is the heat
And the ash and the

Black words that come next.

IV.

Bathysphere

On the Black Sea there is
a city, blackening. There are
buildings quickening, boulevards

bleaching. If you throw your ears
to the sea, if you lose your hands
to sand, you can just make out

rusted hulls and the salt ache
of battlements, empty apartments—
their loneliness. Settling (*sediment*)

like a longing (*childhood*) incurable.
What is concrete what is salt.
Who would ask themselves that?

Pillars and pilings, rush of sand
filling each building's mouth
like a soldier's desperate fingers:

are sandbars now. Are avenues.
Lissome, emptied, atlases.
Violence then sediment then

the cool sobriety of the document.
What is post-Soviet glamour
in photo and video—French boys

will put beats to it, we will nod
our heads to it—is Riviera rubble
and massacre and the Russian genocidaire

now. Palm, pavilion, botanical.

◯

Light and water, light and water,
I step out of the glare, I step
into the cold armament stare

of a more famous coastal
city-state. City of Water, City of Masks,
City of Bridges, City of—

barracks, biennials, slouching
and baroque architectonics.
Paintings curtsey off palazzos

as I drink from slim instruments
and congratulate the artists. In the chill
exhibition hall, opening languidly

as a sleeve, there will be
architectural models—cold,
lapidary, constructed from

internet photographs by eager
assistants—of a bleaching
city, acquiescing to some blacker

sea, somewhere. Not here.
Where my boat writes the canal's
long, inky sentence, villas lean

over to read it, rats tumble
underneath, aquatic. The Yiddish
linguist's famous remark: A language

is a dialect with an army and a navy.
Weaponry, by land and—sea. To whose
language do the buildings belong?

Men with skin the color of molasses,
refugees of the latest "conflict"
just across the water, wander

the national pavilions; they arrived here
by boat. We all did. To such cities
each brings another—other words,

mute to describe other horrors,
other waters. To enter the city (*the poem*)
as one enters the palindrome

and then is stuck. Its hall of mirrors,
of seas, of rivers. Wind lifts up
the white skirts of the waves,

green skirts of the trees, silver sea
of the plaza rocking like a palindrome,
back and forth, back and—

○

The sky some denim. The ocean some
denim. Childhood of palindromes,
poverty of palindromes. The body

an elastic, a respondent, a circle
cometh. Here is another coastal city—
how many are there? Count them.

One, two—here, number three,
a mother is driving her daughter
up a mountain, away from their

ocean, to where the animals live.
This is not to say that the daughter is
an animal, only that she loves them,

as daughters do. She presses
her face to the horses, their sides
like buildings, gleaming

facades warming the arid
evening, and watches her mother's car
leave. Dust, rust-colored, fills the air,

mirroring the road—its simulacra,
a shade. Somewhere far from boots
sinking into stables of orange grove

and eucalyptus, a city is falling, many
cities are falling, to water or to war.
Her mother is falling, sliding down

the mountain in her golden station
wagon to ocean, she catches herself
and speeds off. A girl left to animals,

a mother to her incurables, the horses
to night, mirror-sea that gathers,
its hot breath warming each neck,

words like satellites, foreign
alphabets, strobing the buoyant black.
Which we learn, slow as a language,

from our silvering bathyspheres.

V.

Appenzell

After Robert Walser

I am walking my green hills again. Blue mirrors
of lakes linger like glittery apprentices in their
valleys. In their reflection, I stumble, checking

my collar, dreaming lucidly of ladies in white
dresses that rustle and darken and stain
like so many flowers. The forest describes me

in its verticality, so many pines. Far below
pale sluices of sails prick and slide atop
their blue pools, like my collar. I am thinking

of some steady employment, a grotto, and a motto.
Many young men in service have them. Are attached
to them, like a collar. My throat constricts and I quicken

my steps. It is winter. I am walking my white hills
again, silver mirrors of ice lingering in glittery
apprenticeship to their valleys. In their reflection

I fall, cursing, singing, weeping. In their white
embrace, I lie remembering and remembering
and remembering. We are each the smallest lord,

directing the most minute of sails. We are each
this hill, green then white then dark with my form.

Against Night

Of God, I cry *My body*
and evening shows its back.

Not the voice of cherry trees
greets me, not the low weep

of buildings bending to
the discreet architects of this

looser dark. All around me
windows light softly

as though a thumb dusted
with gold had left its imprint

selectively, each a tepid blessing.
My thoughts tap themselves

out against the amber glass,
restive blue flames that flare

like tiny bodies and disappear.
Should I name these slender

privacies of the soul *sorrow*?
I prepare, with the rest, for

evening's first expulsion.

Autobiographical, Animal, Anaglyph

The curator's quick catechism, the artist's soft inquiry,
pale boats bobbing in a pale sea. The wine wintry

and the summer like a sheet: shook out, shook out, never
to be brought—riding its arch assembly of air currents—

down. Not to me, estranged as concrete, letting blessedly
blind surface suffocate—oh so coldly, tangentally—my cheek.

My eyes slide toward the Rhine's rehearsal, green rivering.
Your small dog like a comma at my feet, strange citation.

Autobiographical, animal, anaglyph: I study its diptych
of wet-lidded bruises for the long lost look of California.

Pictures of you, etc. Nope. Not there, breaststroking
the dark, circular eddies of capillaries. Not there,

focusing the inky pupils with your swarthy presence.
The sun—Swiss, clarion, anticipating some weathery maelstrom

come from the Alpen—checks my eyes too for clues.
What it detects of you, it deflects, or throws away.

The next bather, besuited, bespeckeled, sensibly hides
her eyes behind a pale, winged hand. That breaks the air

like a bird. Then comes the thought, as swimmers blear
the water. Then the memory, as sailors check the mawkish

ping of their sensory. Then the love, as brass bands
pour over the limber bridges: sportif, seismic, adrift.

Instruments, those dark, lush mouths yawning
in the sun, shimmering, then deafening. Your heart

in your mouth, as it were: shimmering, deafening.

Ligurian Tercets

Not patent nor patience
for the chilly lucidity
of this mind's room:

why long walls papered
with slim mint-and-white
stripes of some Riviera

resort of yore, or the dark
and stolid armoire whose
beveled and stained contours

strike S-like poses in the light-
leaving corner? Smoky, silvering
mirrors present so many blue

doubles. As your mind does.
With its long, limber balustrades
and numinous shades.

At which the cat arches her back,
soft dent of paws polarized
by the marble's black-and-white

glare, uxorious grid. If you love
the interior you can stay.
If you loathe the interior

you can stay. The milk-sea
in twilight. The milk-sea
in morning light. Garlands

of salt crystals that glitter
your brow. That glower
and powder and leave pale

trails etched with hikers
who remove their shoes
and like forlorn, antique

clouds, languish then drift
off succulent-strewn cliffs.
Watch them relinquish and

relinquish and relinquish.
From your terrace studded
with hooks, watch them go

O and O and O. Violet stains
steering the sea's surface, restive
shadow that tears, troubles, fames.

Participating Bodies

We waken into a deep freeze.
What are the elements of my disaster?

Cold and the brush fire of your body.
This changes everything.
                              Water rushes

toward the deep swing of torsos.
We are this fissure.

The river that begins in mourning
floods.
          See the sharp slope of jaw,

shifting? The blue
ice of your eye, refracting?

It is everywhere.
I locate you with my mouth.

See my new body?
It paces both sides of the gorge,

limbs loose and flinching
from the roar.

See what we carved?

It twists like a lover
sleeping, long as this October needing.

Fragment

But the tenderness—
                    It could not find us

there, looking out at each other as if from
some dark plain into the disappointing
silver-edged light of our own blindness.

In shadowless winter we were born once,
knew beauty immediately. Saw the snow
stretched out like a beach, the black trees
drawn sharply against it, as the thinner
ebony keys of a piano stand above the ivory.
Heard stillness and reached out to touch it.
The poems came then, came as ice that cut
and trained us. Our tongues split and hands
cracked. In this damaged land we wandered,
damaged *because* of us. If this was our existence

we knew nothing of it. Only: *I* and *You*.
Where are we now? Stay the tenderness,
offer me nothing else. Take my voice
and scratch it cross the ground. Take
our names and throw them back into the pool
of the living. We will lift our faces then,
lift them from the water, lift them to you.

Eucalyptus

You had only just begun loving me
and it shocked you, I think.

Dusk hovering over the quiet gravity of train tracks,

the silver lines stretching into the expectation
of some appearance—this was your voice

saying my name. Anticipation rode your tongue

and I understood *this*, the wound of waiting,
though leaving off the taste of my one

long syllable, you said nothing else.

Love is a plain thing, I think. Along the tracks
a line of eucalyptus breathe heavily

into the night. Everything that has ever hurt you

can be found here. Yet, I am made sharper
by this vague hour, colder. I let the terror

inspect me. I give it a body. In the distance, the bright

freeways wrap around each other but not
for sleep. When the train comes through here

I will be near the water, exacting

from it what we might take from each other,
a world that does not exist, but will.

And To What Do I Not Move?

I came to write your name
in seasons. Snow fields

I let down my hair
for you, calling. Thin

voice threaded through trees,
ribboned against sky;

above me you came,
below me you came,

coatless, dull forelock
and calling my name.

Through my window
I bent to your small figure

on the path below, murmur
of snow tracing your word.

It was our first winter.
Now, windowless, I lean

untoward, and to what
do I not move? Limbs,

fears, all our pleas
and their faces. Through

that room I moved to you
all my places: snowless

beach, river, long grass
shadows, unthroated whisper.

The salt hand in my hair
gives me over. Silently

I curl to ground, dry
leaves burning, faceless.

Like the Augur of an Animal
Across Your Mind

Winter, pewter diorama,
is extinguished. The flora-
embroidered air turns druggy

and new. It stains the fingers.
All down Feldbergstrasse,
houses are heavy with Chinese

wisteria, pendulous purple buds
lewd as grape-stained tongues
wagging over the warring weave

of prewar and postwar—faded
pastel shutters, grimy plastic
grids of windows—each tiny

purple pea the soft suede
of a purse, spending its poisonous
perfume as freely as money. It's spent

on us, lurid scent of the depreciating.
It's spent on the dwellers, the
lovers, the loaners and ladies

of leisure of Feldbergstrasse,
with their Sunday morning walk
to the church so the dog can piss—

on the tulips, on the gothic, on the
perfectly tended-to lawns and latticework—
and call in multiple tongues

the dog to *come here*, its own tongue
unleashing the expected morning
delirium, and unleashing the children

(Turkish, Swiss, French, Italian),
glittery crew of antic syllabics.
Spring is all intimation, and, each year,

a perfect imitation of itself. The tulips,
check. The crocuses, check. The doves
blurring the blue with their calls—

each coo, a check. But for the plum-
colored milk, poison of your wintering
mind, which cloaks each house

with a bell's heaviness, pealing
backwards. Here, flowers strangle
their châteaux. Church gardeners stab

at the earth. Your trespass, your toxin:
that which sorrows in the morning
sun like a dog impervious. Regret,

that seamstress, pulls her thread
tight, her grief accruing like useless
currency, her form wasting from

love lavished too late. Of spring's
previous tenant, your beloved,
you recall a yellow garland of hair

set above wide chloroform eyes.
She was always poor. This presence,
your mother's, lopes like the augur

of an animal across your mind.
Since she will never see this spring,
this season you're in, nor any, not ever

again, you tear off some flowers
from a flinching facade. The buds
shake and tremble, like little bodies

come up from a river. At home, they
lean, they settle, they list along
the vase's studied lip. The room fills

with their scent: lovely, lascivious,
lurid, dead. They bring the outside in.

Order

How many departures have we each
given the other, places as objects in our

decorous order: a street near the beach,
ocean air scoffing at the wary salt

of my tears; a pattern on a sheet
illuminating the disorder of your hair—

Where, on these two coasts, is there
dispassionate room for our ardor,

some parlor stiff enough to counter
my terror? Do they scare you too,

these rooms of sand and sun and books
where our bodies took their leaving

as in a word spoken again to no
effect? I have read that to unlearn

the body its want is the desired order,
autonomous as Eurydice in her poem

who, brushing aside the messenger's arm,
quietly queried, *Who?* There is no more

sober state in which to make such
a claim. What frail and static altar is that,

giving your lover the sight of your
back as you walk without need, and away?

I would not choose lines as lovely
as hers to be mine, though they sift

truth better than any I know. Instead,
I carry the images (*the knowledge*) of

our entrances and exits—marking time
not yet divorced from you—

inside a profane structure much
resembling the armature of my heart,

its tin wires binding deeper
departures of all that continually

bears me back to your name, to you.

The Room in Shadow Does Cast You Out

Could be heard in the fields: my distance
from them. And if my sight made them,
bore them into being every second,
so that they were new, always new—

blond and bending, austere and regarding,
clasped in the sky's loose blue embrace.
Grass a bleached sea sowing itself beneath.
And antelope stunned by heat: sculptural, mercurial.

At the same time this sense of the fields
as existing more painfully than I, did nothing,
created nothing for or from them, it only
did so for me, my want of their being

so obvious that it hung in the blue field
of the sky like a single cloud, hovering,
hungry, unbearingly expressive, with those
slight violet bruises, and my sight—

at once aerial, and yet in line with the horizon's
flame-colored tear, ripping across my eyes—
creating a new feeling at delicate, even
intervals. There I was: new, new, new

again. And the fields, what I had born, been
born of, were also new as the jagged cry
of the firstborn and the very old, or the moth
of seafoam green that suddenly flies to the bulb

lighting the very small white room, and with its
whisper-length of wing, casts an entire cavalry
of dark virtuosity upon the walls, and the room
in shadow does cast you out, into the fields again.

The Flaw

In the small violence of your room
we are eliminated by white.

How do we reach one another?
Not in speech or arrows.

In this narrow bed we lie close.
I take as flaw the windows

and their width, what would call
us far. You are twitching of dreams,

hot as a lamp.
                    Some remote country

takes shape at your temple, a faint
blue river pulsing through it.

This sudden wilderness is where,
without increment, I am made

my feeling for you. Made of it only.

All the while, the fervent light
of morning breathing this into me.

The long, straight windows, from
which I flinch, open hungrily:

a volery seeking the higher
peaks of your chest,
                    touches down—

and flees, immediately.

I follow the shadows it leaves
with my finger. Soon

our bodies will act without
forgiveness,
             and are only

forgiveness—as they gather.

Not the conflict with another, but the
conflict with the world—

            and if you are the world?

Bone China

I lower my breasts into your mouth, one
and then the other.
                        There is no failure
in this giving
if we except everything. Never do this.

I accept the strange blue light
of our pale bodies at night—

a porcelain that absorbs, does not
reflect. We are each a smaller moon

given to the other for brightness.
How I know you now.
                        Coin purse
of your mouth.
The cold clarity of the room

is ceramic, is the clear certainty
of my silver hover above you

            though the mountains

surround us with their animal
prowl, throw back

their black capes
                    and are done.

Our Cavalry Spring

Our cavalry spring finished,
We parted—
At the pair field.

Which lowered
Its streaky head to burnish
Dun and the more damaging gold.

I loved you there. Now
You were gone
Away. Storms approaching

Like dull vertical
Strokes of feeling.
Not like lightning

The quick, remembered birth
Put its hands on me then.
(Its blue of ten-thousand parts

A constant father.)
Like the long tooth of desert
Glittering against the barrel

Chest of sky, highway removed
And removing what felt
For each thing seen—

Blear and overexposed ghosts
Of antelope, fences, posts—
And past. So, I was thinking:

Sky as cloak, field as
Stranger. The economy of such
Comparisons. How they set each

Part to fire. Then a story
Approached, also
Past, but in the horizontal

Form of mountains:
The night I was born
My father left for the desert.

○

Not a story of abandonment,
To be sure, my mother wanted
Him out, and I was not due

For forty-two days (which lined
The sills like rocks taken from water,
Bleaching to rest from some dark

And expert past). Took the truck
From the darkened street that lay
Like a reed along the ocean, and drove

To Death Valley with my uncle, in search
Of a hot spring named, applicably,
Dirty Socks. Not what they wanted: dank,

Deserted, rusted water. Beer cans,
Like abandoned arguments, littering
The edge. Words, like tin, can do that.

Stand at the perimeter and glimmer.
Silence too. Which is how they stood, heat
Like a scavenger, rummaging through

Their dust suits. A local appeared
From the yellow dusk like a thorn. Said
Taking the road farther

Would bring another, more pristine
Spring. Told of heat, of suture, some
Hippies, etc. But the bad road

Narrowed, cacti clawing at tires
That shivered and darkness
Responding until they could see

Nothing and wanted nothing (perhaps).
Then my father saw the woman.
Straight as a match and lit

To a blue tip of flame
By their headlights, she stood
There by the side of the road

With a palomino horse. Of her
My father said: Was tall, with yellow
Hair that burned inside that

Evening's long uncertain
Black hall, was of a beauty
Not—he stopped.

○

And stopped the faded truck.
And feeling words dry false as brush
To their lips, asked of where the springs

Were, of what she was doing
There, silent as a totem born
Of the dust of this road. They didn't say

Deity, totem, we don't understand
What we are doing here. Didn't say
Daughter. She tied her horse

To their truck and joined them,
This nurse sprung like a fierce flag
From the dust. Found the springs

And with her like a knife at their
Side, bathed all night, till I was born.
My father returned, body the emergent

Arrow, to the beach the next morning.
Drove straight out of the desert
Feeling an error had made the world.

This is a common feeling,
I think. And one for which
Trucks and highway are useful.

But my mother met him at
The door, met him with a new
Look, a new body. And upstairs

I began to grow into something
Like that woman at the spring.
Would have horses, would ever

Anticipate some fall. Would wear
The desert like a sign, become
That sign to others. See me and stop,

My animal beside just as silent
As the thing that will make
You halt, make me tie

My horse to your truck,
And take you—*Just a bit
farther*—to the water.

Lupine

I am this drill, this thing,
part and part, parting

like hair. When the mountains
free the animals, when they

finally come down the trail
tied to the gorge like a ribbon,

when they appear from behind the trees
and we see them:

mane, wing, wolf, shake,
then what has been ringing

with sound, will sound
against the gentle trembling

of our legs, the hushed motion
of land before it is felt by hand or hoof.

They, the animals, will lead us by both,
carefully, carefully, lest

we fall against their aching sides,
ask to stop and stop again.

Notes

"Brush Fire" references a line ("My art is colder") from Gang Starr's track "Full Clip" on the album *Full Clip: A Decade of Gang Starr* (1999).

"The Fragments of Swennen" makes use of paintings by Belgian artist Walter Swennen, and is composed, in part, by lines from Dutch art reviews of Swennen's work that have been directly translated into English in Google Translate.

"The Gift" owes a debt to "Sheep in Fog," by Sylvia Plath.

"After-Work Swim at the Thunderbird Motel" refers to the titular motel in Marfa, Texas, as well as to Donald Judd's *100 Untitled Works in Mill Aluminum* (1982–1986), which are on permanent display at the Chinati Foundation, also in Marfa. This poem is for Paolo Thorsen-Nagel.

"Love Comes to the Cracker Factory" alludes to an installation of paintings by Agnes Martin on long-term view at Dia:Beacon, in New York. The poem also refers to the cover image of *Agnes Martin: Writings* (Hatje Cantz, 2005).

"The Eels" is written after a photograph from Francesca Woodman's "Eel Series" (1977–1978), made while the photographer was studying in Rome.

"Chekhov's Photograph" refers to the Anton Chekhov story "The Lady with the Pet Dog," from *The Portable Chekhov* (Penguin, 1977), as well as to the image of the author that graces the cover.

"The Invention" takes its epigraph from a quote by Diane Arbus concerning her 1968 photograph *A Family On Their Lawn One Sunday in Westchester, N.Y.*

"Small Fires" takes its title from *Various Small Fires and Milk* (1964), an artist book of photographs by Ed Ruscha.

"Noon" is written after Ingeborg Bachmann's "Already It's Noon" (trans. Peter Filkins), from *Darkness Spoken: The Collected Poems of Ingeborg Bachmann* (Zephyr Press, 2005).

"Black Words That Come Next" alludes to the Margarete/ Shulamith figure from "Todesfuge" (Deathfugue, trans. John Felstiner) by Paul Celan, and, specifically, the line: "your golden hair Margareta / Your ashen hair Shulamith."

"Bathysphere" takes its title from the Smog song of the same name. The poem makes reference to Sokhumi, a former resort city on the Black Sea that since the ethnic cleansing there in the early 1990s sits in Russian-occupied territory within Georgia's borders. Also evoked are the Yiddish linguist, historian, and translator Max Weinreich (1894–1969); the 54th Venice Biennale; and the "Arab Spring" revolutions in Tunisia, Egypt, Yemen, and Libya that occurred concurrently to the Venice, Italy, exhibition in 2011.

"Appenzell" is written after the Swiss modernist writer Robert Walser, and alludes to an infamous series of police photographs of him taken on Christmas Day, 1956, as he lay dead in the snow in the hills of Eastern Switzerland. The poem also refers to Walser's 1908 novel *The Assistant* (trans. Susan Bernofsky; New Directions, 2007).

"Order" refers to Rainer Maria Rilke's "Orpheus. Eurydice. Hermes" (trans. Stephen Mitchell), from *The Selected Poetry of Rainer Maria Rilke* (Random House, 1982).

And this collection's epigraph is taken from Virginia Woolf's book-length essay *A Room of One's Own* (1929).

Acknowledgments

Many thanks to the editors of the following publications, in which the listed poems, in various forms, originally appeared:

American Poetry Journal: "Fluorescents"
Boston Review: "Brush Fire"
CutBank: "Anticipatory Landscape" and "Slander"
Greensboro Review: "Delineation of Light and Water"
Guernica: "Noon"
The Last Magazine: "Fragment"
Mid-American Review: "Inexpert"
Muthafucka: "Fuel" and "The Fragments of Swennen"
The Paris Review: "Though It Be Foreign, Though It Be Terrible" and "The Eels"
Prairie Schooner: "Intelligence" and "Mineral Violence"
Seneca Review: "Chekhov's Photograph"
Toad: "Diorama," "Idols That Did Call and Call and Call Your Name," "Like the Augur of an Animal Across Your Mind," "My West," and "Order"
Unpleasant Event Schedule: "Short Report on Night"
Vinyl: "Against Night."

Thanks as well to the editors of *Best New Poets 2006*, who reprinted "Chekhov's Photograph"; to the editors of *Verse Daily,* who reprinted "Delineation of Light and Water"; and to the editors of *Vinyl*, who nominated "Against Night" for a Pushcart Prize.

And greatest gratitude to Kolt Beringer, Brandon Shimoda, Anja König, Timothy Donnelly, Richard Howard, and Lucie Brock-Broido for their deft shepherding of so many of these poems, and to J. P. Dancing Bear for thinking them ready for publication. Infinite thanks to Jennifer West and Sarah Leugger for the beautiful cover.

Finally, love and appreciation to my family and friends—West Coast, East Coast, Swiss Coast—for their belief and care; I am so grateful. And to Paolo Thorsen-Nagel.

About the Author

Quinn Latimer was born in 1978 in Venice, California, and educated at Sarah Lawrence College and Columbia University's School of the Arts in New York. Her poems have been featured in *Boston Review, The Paris Review,* and *Prairie Schooner*, among other journals, and recordings or performances of her poems have been included in exhibitions at Art Basel Miami Beach; Galerie J, Geneva; and Kunsthaus Glarus. Latimer currently lives with her husband in Basel, Switzerland, where she regularly contributes criticism about contemporary art and literature to *Artforum, Frieze,* and *Kaleidoscope. Rumored Animals*, which was awarded the 2010 *American Poetry Journal* Book Prize, is her first book.

CPSIA information can be obtained at www.ICGtesting.com
Printed in the USA
LVOW060004260312

274741LV00001B/40/P